ZIMBABWE
‹THE BEAUTIFUL LAND›

ZIMBABWE
‹ THE BEAUTIFUL LAND ›

STRUIK

FRONTISPIECE *The lilacbreasted roller's rainbow colours make it one of the most brightly plumaged of the more than 600 bird species found in Zimbabwe.*

PREVIOUS PAGE *Dust kicked up from parched soil at the end of the dry season rises above a herd of buffalo in Hwange National Park.*

OPPOSITE *Spray soars into the air as the mighty Zambezi River plunges over the Victoria Falls. The bridge across the gorge links the Zimbabwean town of Victoria Falls (in the background) with Livingstone on the Zambian side.*

OVERLEAF *Cheetah on the alert in the grassland of Hwange National Park.*

PAGES 8 & 9 *Grazing impala and the skeletons of trees drowned by the creation of Lake Kariba are silhouetted on Starvation Island.*

Struik Publishers (Pty) Ltd
(a member of The Struik Publishing Group (Pty) Ltd)
Cornelis Struik House
80 McKenzie Street
Cape Town 8001

Reg. No.: 54/00965/07

First published 1991
Second edition 1994
Second impression 1995
Third impression 1997

Copyright © text: Brendan Ryan, 1991, 1994
Copyright © photographs: **Gerald Cubitt**, 1991, 1994 except for the following:
Duncan Butchart (African Images) pages 6/7, 20;
Mike Coppinger page 51 (bottom);
James Marshall (African Images) page 35 (bottom);
Peter Pickford page 30 (top);
Peter Steyn pages 19 (bottom), 21 (top and bottom), 33, 67;
Mark van Aardt main cover photograph, cover (middle inset);
Zimbabwe Sun Hotels page 15 (bottom);
Zimbabwe Tourist Development Corporation pages 11 (top), 13 (bottom),
   14 (bottom), 76 (bottom).
Copyright in the abovementioned photographs remains with the individual photographers.

Layout by Janine Poezyn
Typesetting by Diatype Setting cc, Cape Town
Reproduction by Unifoto (Pty) Ltd, Cape Town
Printed and bound by Kyodo Printing Co (Singapore) Pte Ltd

ISBN 1 86825 556 5

TOP *Still waters reflect the Troutbeck Inn at Nyanga – one of a number of hotels in the Eastern Highlands that offer guests relaxed country living in a scenic setting.*

ABOVE *Bougainvillea and aloes flourish in the Ewanrigg Botanical Garden, about 40 km from Harare. The garden is best visited between June and August, when the winter-flowering aloes blaze with colour.*

INTRODUCTION

Zimbabwe is a country where you can experience the thrill of white-water rafting in the gorges below the world's greatest waterfall; where you can stalk elephant on foot armed with only a camera; and where you can take on the tigerfish – a razor-toothed scrapper whose fighting qualities are legendary amongst anglers.

It is also a land of spectacular landscapes, where erosion over millions of years has created from the unusual geology a rugged beauty that has to be seen to be really appreciated. Over an area covering nearly half of Zimbabwe's 389 000-km² extent the underlying granite has been exposed to the elements – and nowhere more dramatically than in the Matobo Hills near Bulawayo. This 320 000-ha region is made up almost entirely of huge, dome-like granite hills called whalebacks and weirdly shaped balancing rock formations known as castle kopjes. In the east a series of rugged mountain ranges known collectively as the Eastern Highlands forms the border with Mozambique, while to the north one of Africa's greatest rivers, the Zambezi, contributes the most stunning sight of all – the Victoria Falls. Dammed further along its course, the Zambezi forms another scenic wonder in Lake Kariba, one of the world's largest man-made lakes.

Although the magnificent scenery is, without doubt, a major attraction, it is the chance to experience some of Africa's last great wilderness regions that draws visitors back to Zimbabwe again and again. This country offers game-viewing second to none. Some 11,5 per cent of its land area has been set aside for conservation purposes and designated national park, safari area or recreation area. Called the Parks and Wildlife Estate, this protected land is administered by the Department of National Parks and Wildlife Management (National Parks).

Conservation is taken seriously here, although the effects of recent cutbacks in Government funding are starting to show. Nevertheless, Zimbabwe is one of the very few countries in Africa where the elephant population has increased in the past few years. It also has the infrastructure to cater for all types of wildlife enthusiast, whether he likes to do his game-viewing in five-star luxury or prefers to slog it out on a wilderness trail in 40 °C heat and a cloud of tsetse flies.

Accommodation in the national parks is varied and includes fully equipped lodges, cottages and chalets with communal ablution facilities, and camping sites. In the major national parks, such as Hwange, all these types of accommodation are provided, whereas in the more remote ones, such as Matusadona, only camping sites or a very limited number of lodges – as at Mana Pools – are available. Whatever the facilities, the camps are invariably well run and the members of staff are helpful.

The steadily growing number of tourists visiting Zimbabwe has triggered a mini boom in the local safari industry and a large number of companies now offer trips into the 'bush' for visitors unable to travel there on their own. These safaris range from standard ones in four-wheel-drive vehicles to canoe expeditions along the Zambezi River. Exclusive camps offering luxury accommodation are also being run by private safari operators on the borders of the national parks as well as on private game ranches. Controlled hunting is an integral part of Zimbabwe's conservation programme and some companies offer their clients the opportunity to hunt in safari areas under the jurisdiction of the Department of National Parks and Wildlife Management or on private land. In both cases quotas of animals that may be shot are set and the hunting is strictly monitored.

The country's largest national park – and one of the finest in Africa – is the 14 500-km² Hwange National Park which lies about 250 km north-west of Bulawayo, just off the main road to the Victoria Falls. This vast, sometimes desolate-looking reserve supports large herds of buffalo and elephant, as well as black and white rhino, and 16 antelope species which include sable, roan and gemsbok. Giraffe browse throughout the park, and herds of zebra can often be seen at the waterholes. Although lion, leopard, cheetah, wild dog and hyena also occur, they are more difficult to spot. More than 300 bird species have been identified in Hwange, and birdwatchers will almost certainly find a slow drive along any of the park's roads rewarding. Of the four public camps, Main Camp is the largest and most easily accessible. Sinamatella – perched on a ridge with a magnificent view across the plains below – Robins and Nantwich are more intimate and seem to blend into the bush.

Just an hour or so's drive from Hwange lie the Victoria Falls, Zimbabwe's prime tourist attraction. It is impossible to put into words the effect that this stupendous, falling sheet of water has on those who gaze on it. Some 1,7 km wide and with an average height of about 97 m, it flings up spray hundreds of metres into the air. Like most of the country's natural assets, the Falls are delightfully undeveloped – all there is to detract from the natural state is a paved footpath that follows the lip of the gorge, allowing the visitor to wander through the rain forest from viewpoint to viewpoint.

The adjacent town boasts several good hotels as well as two campsites, and there are self-catering lodges in the nearby Victoria Falls National Park. A major attraction for many visitors is to go white-water rafting below the Falls – it's rated one of the most exhilarating river rides in the world.

Beyond the Victoria Falls the Zambezi flows eastwards for about 100 km before it enters Lake Kariba – the vast man-made lake formed in the late 1950s by the construction of a dam wall at Kariba Gorge. Nearly 300 km in length from its westernmost point to the dam wall, the lake is 42 km across at the widest part and has an average depth of 18 m. Hotel development at the town of Kariba has created an inland riviera which offers activities such as water-skiing, paragliding and boating. This is one of Zimbabwe's premier holiday resorts, where an elephant reluctant to move out of the road is more likely to cause a traffic jam than vehicle congestion.

On the southern shore of the lake, opposite the town, lies arguably Zimbabwe's finest national park – Matusadona. Along the edge of the lake the flood waters have created a unique landscape of dead trees standing skeleton-like in the water. When combined with the flaming crimson sunsets for which the lake is noted, this area becomes a photographer's nirvana. A number of luxury safari and fishing resorts are situated along the national park's shore and on nearby islands, and these are best reached by boat or small aircraft. The many inlets along the shore shelter tigerfish which can attain weights of up to 12 kg, although fish of around 5 kg are more common. Even the most experienced fishermen expect to lose up to five 'tigers' for every one landed; these fish are adept at breaking line or throwing hooks in the tail-walking rush and aerial gymnastics that invariably follow a strike.

Below Kariba the river emerges from the gorge and flows towards another superb national park – Mana Pools – so named for the pools created on a broad floodplain which was inundated frequently by the Zambezi before the dam wall was built. This is another unforgettable landscape, created by the extensive forests of *Acacia albida* trees growing on the floodplain. Mana Pools is noted particularly for its elephants, which feed on the *Acacia albida* seed pods during the late winter months and are often seen browsing on the islands in mid-stream.

Open to the public only from May to October, the park teems with game such as buffalo, lion, hippo and a vast array of plains antelope – including eland, kudu, bushbuck and waterbuck. Crocodile, common everywhere along the Zambezi, lurk along the river's banks, posing a threat to the unwary. Visitors are allowed to walk through this wilderness unaccompanied, strictly at their own risk, but can, if they prefer, take a

TOP *Displays of African tribal dancing are a regular attraction for tourists at Victoria Falls.*

ABOVE *Zimbabwe is internationally renowned for crafts such as sculpture and pottery. This display of earthenware is from the Chiredzi region in the south-east.*

TOP *Safari minibuses leave Hwange National Park's Main Camp on a game-viewing drive.*

CENTRE *Ferry passengers prepare to disembark at Mlibizi, at the western end of Lake Kariba, after a 22-hour journey from Kariba.*

ABOVE *Guided walks are a feature of many of Zimbabwe's national parks. They are led by safari guides – as shown here at Chikwenya, downstream of Mana Pools – or by a parks ranger.*

guided walk led by an experienced National Park game scout. Many safari companies run tours into Mana Pools, the main camp, Nyamepi, being a favoured base as it is the centre for the highly popular canoe safaris. Trips along the Zambezi from Chirundu to Mana Pools can last up to a week, and then continue on down to the Mozambique border at Kanyemba. Because Mana Pools is surrounded by safari hunting areas, this entire stretch of river, more than 200 km long, flows through wilderness. Canoeing aficionados claim there is no better way to view game because you can get close to animals drinking at the water's edge – they do not seem to associate boats with the normal threats posed by man.

This region has also been the testing ground for Zimbabwe's commitment to conservation, as it has borne the brunt of an invasion of poachers from Zambia. The largest population of black rhino remaining in the wild occurs in the Zambezi Valley, and it is these endangered animals, with their sought-after horn, that are the poachers' target. They have been virtually eradicated from the rest of Africa north of Zimbabwe, but here the outcome of the war between conservation authorities and the poachers is still in the balance. Rhino and elephant poachers are shot on sight, and although scores have been killed in recent years the rhino population has suffered severely. Once common at Mana Pools, rhino are now rarely seen, and elephant, too, are coming under increasing pressure from poachers.

After the heat of the 'Valley' – as the Zambezi River area is generally termed – the cooler, misty forested country of the Eastern Highlands is another world. Tigerfish and baobabs are exchanged for trout, tree ferns and msasa trees. There are three main sections to this 200-km long stretch of mountains: Nyanga in the north, the Vumba in the centre near the region's main city, Mutare, and the Chimanimani in the south.

Nyanga is a region of open, moor-like country dominated by nearby peaks which include the nation's highest – Mount Inyangani at 2 592 m. It can be explored on foot or horseback, or by following a network of gravel roads. Specially bred trout provide sport for anglers in the rivers and dams, and several of the excellent hotels have golf courses. Nyanga National Park covers much of the area and offers self-catering accommodation in lodges alongside some of the dams, as well as a camping site. The ruins of early settlements dot the region, and of these perhaps the most intriguing is the Van Niekerk complex, which covers more than 80 km² and comprises stone terracing, pits and forts. There is a military base nearby, so it is wise to confirm access to the complex with the national park warden.

Mutare, surrounded by mountains and lying just north-west of the Vumba, is one of the prettiest cities in southern Africa. Views from several lookout points around the town are spectacular, and best enjoyed in August and September when the msasa trees come into leaf, spreading a patchwork of red, crimson, copper and rust shades over the hillsides before they turn a delicate green. The Vumba area is lusher than Nyanga, and the forests and Botanical Garden are a must for birdwatchers. Here rare bird species restricted to the Eastern Highlands and neighbouring Mozambique are most easily seen.

Further south lie the Chimanimani Mountains, a largely undeveloped area which can only be explored on foot. The road into Chimanimani National Park ends at the park's base camp, where rudimentary camping facilities are provided. From there it's a three-hour hike up to a simple refuge hut in the mountains, a base for exploring the full range. Take care not to wander into Mozambique – there are no border posts up here.

South-west of Chimanimani, near the town of Masvingo, lie the massive ruins of Great Zimbabwe. The centre of a civilisation, this stone-walled city flourished for hundreds of years before its sudden and mysterious decline in the fifteenth century. Enough still stands of the once-magnificent city to awe the visitor, its dry-stone granite walls blending with the surrounding landscape. In these ruins were found the soapstone Zimbabwe birds which have become the symbol of the new nation. Although by far the most impressive complex of ruins in the country, Great Zimbabwe is just one of many such reminders of this bygone civilisation. Other extensive ruins are located at Nyanga, at Kame near Bulawayo, and at Dhlo Dhlo and Nalatale near Gweru – to mention a few.

Another, earlier culture which has made a valuable contribution to Zimbabwe's heritage is that of the San or Bushmen, whose artists used the country's granite-walled caves as canvases on which to document their world. At its best, Bushman art fills any naturalist with wonder at how the artists, using such a crude medium, could capture so well the essential grace of an animal such as a kudu. Examples of their work can be seen in thousands of sites throughout Zimbabwe, the most accessible of which are in the Matobo Hills near Bulawayo and at Domboshawa near Harare. In the Matobo the many caves containing Bushman paintings add an extra dimension of interest to a landscape that is unique. Matobo in Ndebele means 'bald heads' and is an apt description of the massive grey granite whalebacks which dominate the area.

The Bushmen were driven out of Zimbabwe by the iron-age builders of the stone-walled cities, a more sophisticated people who migrated into southern Africa and occupied Zimbabwe around the eleventh century. Based on farming cattle and mining for gold and iron, their civilisation here flourished so well that they had the time to devote to the construction of their stone-walled cities. They also had contact with the outside world through Arab traders. Middle Eastern and Chinese artefacts found in the various ruins by archeologists can be seen in Bulawayo's excellent national museum. After the decline of Great Zimbabwe other stone-walled cities such as Kame and Dhlo Dhlo took precedence at various times. The descendants of the tribes who lived in them – such as the Karanga and the Rozvi – form the vast majority of Zimbabwe's approximately 9 million population and are known today as the Shona people.

An Arab trader was probably the first non-African to see Zimbabwe; the first known written mention of the region was by the Arab traveller Masudi in the tenth century. From about 1500 onwards the first Europeans to penetrate into the country were the Portuguese, who probed inland from a series of shipping posts set up on the Mozambique coast. Lured, inevitably, by rumours of gold, they mistakenly believed that the gold mines and stone-walled cities of Zimbabwe were the source of the biblical King Solomon's wealth. Like many an eager gold hunter in later times, they were to be sadly disappointed.

Although dealings with the Arabs and Portuguese were complicated, the Shona enjoyed a fairly peaceful existence until the beginning of the nineteenth century. Then their world was turned upside down by raiding tribes from the south. The origins of this upheaval have been traced back to the Zululand region of present-day South Africa, where Shaka was consolidating his grip on what would become the Zulu nation. In 1819 he defeated his main rival, Zwide, whose tribe disintegrated. Some of Zwide's followers fled northwards in three splinter groups, the first of which, led by a chief called Zwangendaba, rampaged through Zimbabwe in 1826. The local tribes were no match for the warrior bands who destroyed much of their civilisation, looting many of the stone-walled cities. Zwangendaba's group was followed by the other two splinter armies and over a period of some years they reduced the Shona tribes to a state of destitution.

Meanwhile, events in Zululand were about to unleash an even worse foe on the Shona – Mzilikazi and his followers, who became known as the Ndebele or Matabele. Mzilikazi fled Zululand in 1822 to avoid death at the hands of Shaka and settled initially in the highveld region of what is now

TOP *Spurwing Island, one of the luxury camps on Lake Kariba.*

CENTRE *Drivers new to Zimbabwe very quickly learn an essential rule of the road – elephants have right of way.*

ABOVE *Sikumi Tree Lodge, a private luxury camp at Hwange National Park.*

TOP *The statue of explorer David Livingstone – the first European to see the Victoria Falls – is situated close enough to the Devil's Cataract at the Falls to be soaked by spray.*

ABOVE *The centre of Harare, Zimbabwe's capital, with a summer thunderstorm brewing on the horizon.*

the Transvaal province of South Africa. However, a combination of raids by the Zulus and confrontations with the Voortrekkers – the white pioneers who were at that time pushing into the Transvaal from the Cape – drove him across the Limpopo River and as far north as the site of the present-day city of Bulawayo. He set himself up as king over what is now the province of Matabeleland and from here his armies raided and plundered at will the long-suffering Shona tribes.

In 1853 Mzilikazi signed a treaty with the Voortrekkers in the Transvaal, part of which provided for safe passage for hunters and traders into his domain. From then on a growing number of white hunters started to explore the country north of the Limpopo. With them came prospectors, some of whom found not only traces of gold, but also the old Shona mine workings; their reports aroused growing interest in the region.

Mzilikazi died in 1868 and was succeeded by Lobengula, who continued the friendly policy towards the white newcomers. From about 1880 interest in the land controlled by the Ndebele soared as the scramble for Africa by various European powers gained momentum. One man in particular – mining magnate and British imperialist Cecil John Rhodes – focussed his attention on Lobengula's realm.

Constantly petitioned by concession seekers, in February 1888 Lobengula signed the so-called 'Moffat Treaty' by which he agreed not to commit himself to any contracts or treaties without British approval. In October of the same year he signed the Rudd Concession which granted the holders exclusive rights to metals and minerals in his kingdom, this being defined in the agreement to include the land occupied by the Shona tribes. Rhodes used this document – which was solely a mineral rights agreement – as the basis from which to take over Lobengula's land. In October 1889 he obtained a Royal Charter to form the British South Africa Company (BSA Company) which was granted nearly all administrative responsibilities over, and commercial land rights in, the region.

A pioneer column of settlers and military personnel crossed the Shashe River at Tuli in July 1890 and, after carefully skirting Matabeleland, headed for the heart of Mashonaland. It reached the site of the present city of Harare on 12 September 1890 and set up Fort Salisbury. Lobengula, extremely unhappy about these developments, fought the pioneers in 1893 but was put to flight when the latter occupied Bulawayo on 4 November that year. He died on his retreat northwards, and the BSA Company took over Matabeleland, effectively running the country that was to be known from then until 1980 as Rhodesia. Bulawayo became a boom town, although the hard facts of the country's geology soon became apparent – gold traces were plentiful, but there were no deposits even remotely like the treasure house that had been uncovered further south on the Witwatersrand.

Occupation of the country by the pioneers did not go uncontested; in 1896 the Matabele rose in rebellion and, in what is now known as the first war of liberation, the Shona followed suit. Both rebellions were overcome, but Matabele resistance continued until Rhodes himself intervened and negotiated with the leaders. The British government confirmed the authority of the BSA Company to run the country and, represented by a High Commissioner, retained limited powers for itself. The Company remained in control until October 1923 when the Rhodesians voted for self-government and against an alternative proposal to join the Union of South Africa. From that point Britain and the Rhodesians diverged in their approach to racial matters; the latter went their own way, although technically they remained the responsibility of Britain.

The Federation of the Rhodesias and Nyasaland was formed in 1953, bringing together Southern Rhodesia, Northern Rhodesia (now Zambia) and Nyasaland (now Malawi). It lasted 10 uneasy years, but was finally dissolved by Britain in response to growing pressure from African nationalists. In 1964 Britain granted independence based on majority rule to Zambia and Malawi, but refused it to Southern Rhodesia because of disagreement over franchise rights. The following year, on 11 November, the minority government led by Ian Smith declared unilateral independence; the country was immediately subjected to international economic sanctions. Armed resistance by nationalist leaders – the second war of liberation – started on a small scale in 1966 and then escalated dramatically into a bitter civil war that lasted from 1972 to 1980. By then the war and economic sanctions had brought the country to its knees and forced the Lancaster House agreement that brought independence under majority rule. The current ruling Zanu PF party of executive president Robert Mugabe was voted to power in the subsequent elections, and the new nation of Zimbabwe came into being on 17 April 1980.

Since then the country has recovered from the effects of the war and is peaceful except for certain areas on its border with Mozambique, a country still in the throes of civil war. Gona-re-zhou National Park, in the south-east, was closed to tourists for several years because of the security situation there, but at the time of publication is gradually being re-opened.

Visitors to Zimbabwe will find the people to be generally friendly and helpful, and a courteous approach to authorities such as the police, customs and immigration will invariably be replied to in kind. The tourism industry in Zimbabwe maintains high standards, with excellent hotels in all the major tourist centres as well as in Harare and Bulawayo. Visitors travelling the country under their own steam will find a wide and plentiful range of groceries, fresh meat and vegetables in the local shops, but shortages of certain items do occur from time to time. Tourists are advised, for example, to bring with them all the camera film they will need.

The country's main roads are bliss to drive on because they are well maintained and carry relatively little traffic. Financial restrictions on the importing of cars over the past three decades, as well as a current shortage of foreign exchange, have kept the number of vehicles in Zimbabwe low. A disadvantage, however, is that the lack of spare parts results in poor vehicle maintenance, and motorists should watch out for cars and trucks without head- or tail-lights, or without indicators. This, as well as stray livestock and wild game on the roads, makes travelling at night hazardous.

Malaria is prevalent throughout Zimbabwe – particularly in the lowveld areas – and visitors are advised to take anti-malaria tablets. They should also guard against contracting bilharzia, an unpleasant disease acquired through contact with infected water. The cold, fast-flowing streams of the Eastern Highlands are the only waters that can be considered safe.

Zimbabwe's climate is superb, even during the dry winter months when in the central highveld and middleveld regions temperatures are usually about 25 °C during the day. Nights are cool, and frost seldom occurs. In summer the temperatures in these areas range from 30 to 35 °C and the rain normally results from short, violent thunderstorms. The lowveld areas, which include the entire Zambezi Valley, are another matter in summer, when temperatures soar to well above 40 °C during the day and remain high at night. In winter temperatures in the Valley are slightly higher than in the highveld region and the evenings are pleasant. Generally cooler conditions prevail in the Eastern Highlands, where the mountains create their own wet and unpredictable weather patterns.

At the end of a journey through Zimbabwe visitors take away with them unforgettable images of the mesmeric power and beauty of Victoria Falls, of sunset reflected on the still waters of Lake Kariba, perhaps of a lion crouched in sun-bleached grass or elephant playing at the water's edge. Photographer and wildlife enthusiast, sun-worshipper and sightseer, all will have indelible memories of this beautiful land.

TOP *Tree ferns are a dominant feature in the Vumba Botanical Gardens, one of the finest in Zimbabwe. Some 32 ha of the 201-ha site have been developed and the entire area is a delight for botanist and birdwatcher.*

ABOVE *The gracious elegance of the Victoria Falls Hotel, which has been catering for guests since 1904.*

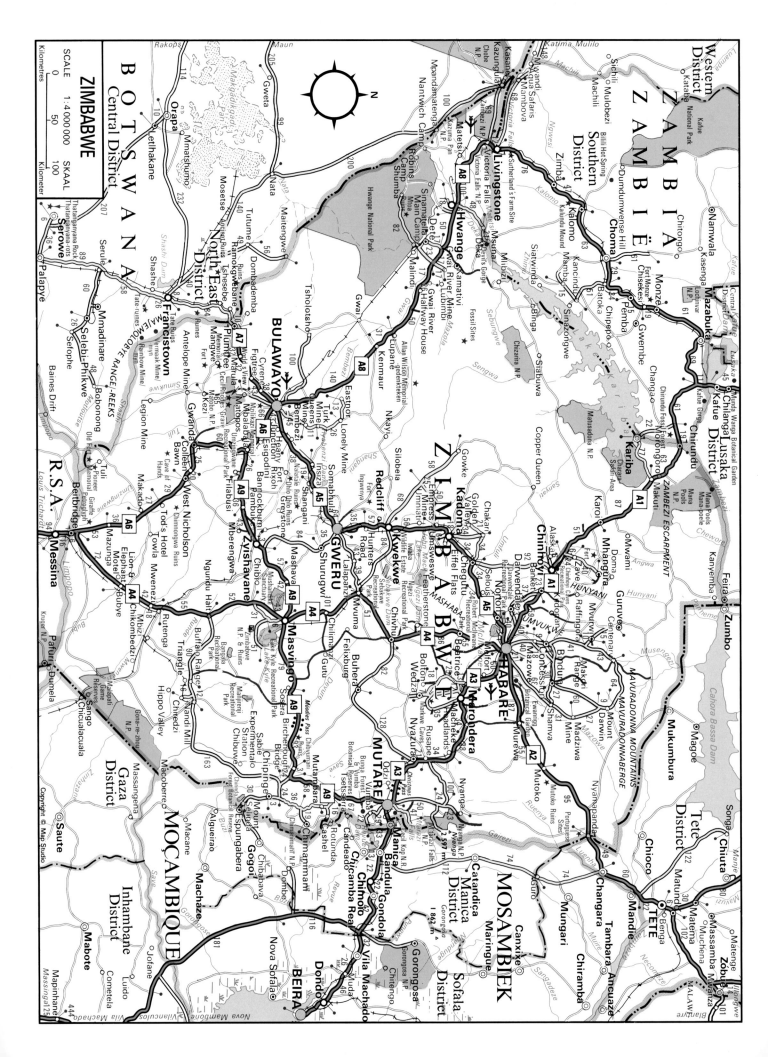

RIGHT *The Great Enclosure of the Zimbabwe Ruins, which lie just south of Lake Kyle. Covering a site of some 720 ha, the ancient city had between 11 000 and 20 000 inhabitants at any given time during its heyday.*

PREVIOUS PAGE *Zebra are common in Hwange National Park and are readily seen, although their dramatic black and white striping blends in surprisingly well with the surroundings.*

ABOVE *Lake Kyle, the second largest dam in Zimbabwe, was built to supply the huge sugar cane and other agricultural projects in the south-eastern district. The level of the lake has been seriously affected by drought in recent years.*

LEFT *The Conical Tower within the Great Enclosure is one of the main features of the ruins, yet its symbolic meaning remains open to conjecture.*

ABOVE *Granite boulders balance on a 'whaleback' in the Matobo Hills near Bulawayo. Over millions of years erosion has exposed the underlying granite, carving away weak rock strata and weathering large blocks into rounded boulders which will eventually tumble to the base of the 'whaleback'.*

RIGHT ABOVE *A black eagle on its nest site in the Matobo Hills. These birds of prey are common in the area, where they feed on the abundant dassie population.*

RIGHT BELOW *A mosaic of Bushman paintings covers the granite wall of this cave in the Matobo.*

ABOVE *A young kudu bull peers from cover in Hwange National Park. When it reaches maturity its horns will have grown into magnificent spirals with up to two and a half twists.*

LEFT *Evening sun reflects off the dust kicked up by a herd of buffalo coming down to drink at the Caterpillar Pan near Hwange's Main Camp.*

LEFT *One of Hwange's 'clown princes' — a yellowbilled hornbill. These distinctive birds have become very tame at some of the waterholes and will readily try to scrounge food from visitors. Feeding birds or animals in the park is not permitted.*

FAR LEFT *Nature's skyscrapers — a giraffe duo in the Hwange National Park, where these elegant creatures are frequently seen browsing at treetop level or stooping to drink at the waterholes and pans.*

BELOW *Two young buffalo bulls playfully try out their considerable strength.*

ABOVE *Nature red in tooth and claw. A lioness and her cubs feed on the remains of a buffalo she killed at Hwange's Makwa Pan.*

ABOVE RIGHT *Feeding time for a zebra foal. The bond between mare and foal is very close and only begins to loosen when the latter weans at about 11 months old.*

OVERLEAF *The dust flies as a herd of buffalo stampedes away from danger in Hwange National Park.*

ABOVE *A typical 'mixed bag' gathers to drink at Hwange's Nyamandhlovu Pan
— sable, zebra and giraffe.*

LEFT ABOVE *The bateleur is one of the most common — and, with its distinctive
plumage and flight action, most easily recognised — raptors at Hwange.*

LEFT BELOW *A white rhino and her calf in a Hwange thicket. At one time
exterminated from this area by hunters, both the black and the white rhino have
been reintroduced and are occasionally seen in the park.*

ABOVE *A blackbacked jackal — ever an opportunist and scavenger — takes a break for a quick drink.*

LEFT *A herd of elephant drinking at Detema dam in the western section of Hwange, between Sinamatella and Robins camps.*

ABOVE *Waterbuck cool off in a dam at Hwange. These shaggy-coated antelope are highly dependent on water and never roam far from a water supply, even if it is an artificial one.*

ABOVE RIGHT *A spitting lion cub plays 'king of the castle' on a convenient termite mound. Lions are social animals, and interaction between cubs forms an important part of their development.*

RIGHT *Leopard are found throughout Hwange, but are rarely seen on account of their secretive, and largely nocturnal, habits.*

ABOVE *Robins Camp, in the western sector of Hwange, nestles in a sea of surrounding mopane bush. The camp is usually closed from 1 November to 30 April, when the rains make a number of the roads in this part of the park impassable to ordinary vehicles.*

LEFT *Treehouse accommodation at the bush camp run by the Hwange Safari Lodge. A limited number of guests may overnight at the bush camp, where they experience Hwange's nightlife at close hand.*

ABOVE *Impala are Hwange's most common antelope and herds of 20 or more are frequently seen. The herd ram, with his lyre-shaped horns, is lying down in the left foreground.*

LEFT *One of Zimbabwe's many small predators — a serval cat — is caught and photographically on the ground during the day.*

ABOVE *Sunrise on a tranquil Zambezi River just upstream of the Victoria Falls. In geographical terms the Zambezi at this point is in its placid mature stage, but the plunge over the Falls rejuvenates it.*

LEFT ABOVE *A waterbuck ram in the Victoria Falls National Park. This handsome antelope is found near rivers or lakes in most of Zimbabwe's national parks.*

LEFT BELOW *Sable are regularly seen in the Victoria Falls National Park which extends along the Zambezi River upstream of the Falls.*

OVERLEAF *The width of the Victoria Falls, from Devil's Cataract (centre) to the Eastern Cataract on the Zambian side, is 1,7 km. Regular flights over the Falls every day allow visitors to get an overall perspective on this scenic wonder.*

ABOVE *Sightseers board a launch for a trip on the Zambezi above the Falls.*

ABOVE RIGHT *A trumpeter hornbill perches above the canopy of the rain forest at Victoria Falls. Zimbabwe's second largest hornbill, this magnificent bird is common in forests along the Zambezi River.*

LEFT *Young crocodiles in the crocodile ranch at Victoria Falls. Commercial farming of these reptiles has greatly boosted their populations in the wild, as a certain number has to be released into the Zambezi annually.*

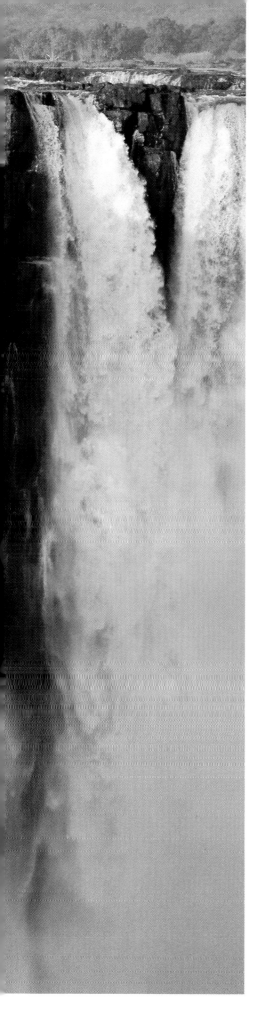

ABOVE *A rainbow shimmers across the Falls in this view taken from the Devil's Cataract looking eastwards.*

LEFT *The Zambezi River plunges over the main section of the Victoria Falls. The annual average flow of water over the Falls is 340 000 cubic metres a minute, with peak floods occurring during April and the lowest flow in November.*

ABOVE *A bushbuck poses delicately in the rain forest at the Victoria Falls. These normally timid antelope are often seen by visitors walking along the paths that link the various viewpoints overlooking the Falls.*

RIGHT *The Zambezi boils and churns in the Devil's Cataract.*

ABOVE *An aerial view of the Victoria Falls, taken from upstream. The start of the series of gorges through which the Zambezi flows below the Falls can be seen in the background to the left.*

ABOVE RIGHT *The lush rain forest, created by persistent spray from the Falls, is no more than a few hundred metres wide. Where the spray no longer reaches the vegetation suddenly reverts to dry bushveld.*

RIGHT *One for the brave . . . white-water rafting in the gorges below the Falls.*

OVERLEAF *Impala gather on the shoreline at Matusadona National Park. September and October are good months for game-viewing at Lake Kariba as the heat builds up before the rains and the herds of game spend more time near the water.*

ABOVE *Lake Kariba is the haunt of a diversity of waterbirds, including colourful saddlebilled storks which stand a metre and a half high.*

LEFT *One of the best ways to explore the Matusadona shore of Lake Kariba is by houseboat. While the boat is anchored in a quiet, remote bay such as this one, a small motorboat can be used to go fishing or game-viewing.*

LEFT BELOW *Pink jacaranda* (Stereospermum kunthianum) *trees in blossom bring a delicate splash of colour to the dry hillsides around Kariba in August and September.*

ABOVE *Elephant straggle along the Kariba shore; a supply of clean fresh water is an essential requirement for them, and if necessary they will travel considerable distances to drink.*

RIGHT *A fish eagle, a common sight at Lake Kariba, drops its hard-won catch.*

ABOVE *White skeletons of drowned trees dot a shallow bay offshore of the Matusadona National Park. The changing level of the lake sometimes hides, sometimes reveals tree stumps just below the surface, and boat pilots must navigate through these areas with extreme caution.*

RIGHT ABOVE *The wall of Kariba Dam was completed in 1959 to generate hydroelectricity for both Zimbabwe and Zambia. Visitors may walk onto the wall from the Zimbabwean side after having reported to the Zimbabwe immigration post.*

RIGHT BELOW *A pair of kapenta fishing boats return to harbour at Kariba after a night's work. Kapenta – a type of freshwater sardine – were introduced to the lake and now form the basis of a substantial fishing industry. The tiny fish are attracted to the surface at night by bright lights and are then scooped up in the circular nets.*

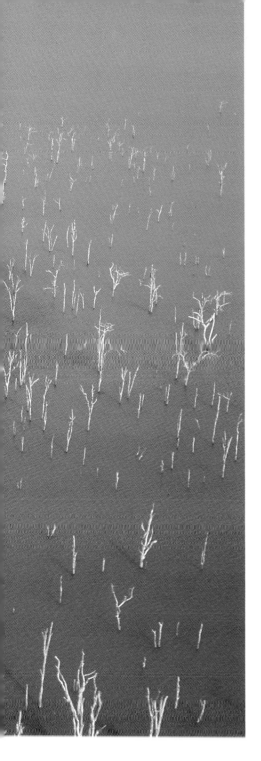

ABOVE A herd of Zimbabwe's most common antelope, impala, on Starvation Island, near Bumi Hills.

FAR LEFT Elephant watering from Lake Kariba. These animals should be treated with caution at all times — keep a respectful distance even if you are in a vehicle.

LEFT A stately male waterbuck displays his trademarks: a fine set of curving horns and the white ring on his rump.

OVERLEAF A huge herd of buffalo grazes along the shoreline of the Matusadona National Park at Lake Kariba. The changing level of the water in the lake has created extensive grasslands along its shores.

ABOVE *A game-viewing hide on the Matusadona shore. The recent high-water level reached by the lake can be seen on the tree trunk below the hide.*

ABOVE RIGHT *Below Kariba Gorge the Zambezi River slows to a leisurely pace, interrupted by numerous sandbanks and islands as it winds towards Mana Pools.*

RIGHT *A solitary grey heron stands alert, watching for any movement that would betray its next meal.*

ABOVE *A sight to set the adrenalin flowing in the veins of even the most intrepid canoeist. Hippo abound in the Zambezi and members of canoe safaris treat them with utmost respect.*

ABOVE RIGHT *From September to November the riverbanks along the Zambezi are alive with breeding colonies of carmine bee-eaters.*

ABOVE *Yellowbilled storks forage on an island in the Zambezi River near Mana Pools.*

LEFT *An elephant bull checks the wind, suspicious of his surroundings. Visitors may walk unaccompanied at Mana Pools if they wish, but should never forget that all wildlife can be dangerous.*

RIGHT *An increasingly rare sight in the Zambezi Valley – a black rhino ponders fight or flight. Poaching continues to take a heavy toll of these endangered animals.*

ABOVE *At Mana Pools buffalo dot the landscape, which is dominated by huge Acacia albida trees. By the end of the dry season the teeming game herds at Mana Pools have eaten most of the grass on the plains.*

ABOVE LEFT *No visitor dare forget that crocodiles are an ever-present menace in the Zambezi, as recent attacks on unwary anglers and canoeists attest.*

OVERLEAF *A herd of impala picks its way through Acacia forest near the luxury Chikwenya safari camp.*

LEFT *World's View in Nyanga National Park. From here the escarpment drops some 700 m into the subtropical valleys below.*

FAR LEFT *In August and September msasa trees colour the countryside below the Inyangombe Falls in Nyanga National Park.*

LEFT BELOW *Getting away from it all with some quiet fishing on the lake at the Troutbeck Inn near Nyanga.*

ABOVE *The dry, rolling countryside of Nyanga forms a backdrop to the springtime colours of the msasa trees.*

ABOVE LEFT *The Pungwe River creates a spectacular waterfall where it tumbles off the Nyanga escarpment.*

LEFT *Mist rises through pine forests in the Eastern Highlands. Extensive tracts of land have been planted with exotic trees such as pine and wattle for Zimbabwe's timber, pulp and paper industries.*

ABOVE Leucospermum saxosum *in the Chimanimani mountains. The climate and terrain of this mountainous region are not unlike those of South Africa's south-western Cape Province, and many fynbos species found there also flourish in this south-eastern corner of Zimbabwe.*

RIGHT *The Bridal Veil Falls at Chimanimani are regarded by many to be the most beautiful in Zimbabwe. The veil effect is created by the falling column of water hitting a series of closely spaced steps in the rock face.*

*A massive baobab stands sentinel-like next to the main road into Kariba.
These trees are found only in the hot, low-lying regions of Zimbabwe.*